Introduction

Creating cross-stitch masterpieces for the holidays is so much fun. So many people enjoy stitching but find that finishing time is short and ideas hard to come by. Enter perforated paper. This stitching medium, which first became available in the early 19th century, has been a go-to material for stitchers for nearly 200 years. Victorians used perforated paper for making bookmarks, cards and even needlebooks before the trend faded in the early 20th century. However, designers have resurrected this medium and livened it up for today's stitcher with contemporary colors, designs and finishes. This book is dedicated to perforated-paper designs and features projects that are both trendy and timeless. In this book, you will find beautiful designs to hang on your walls, adorable ornaments to hang on your holiday tree, and unique projects to display on your mantel or side table throughout the Christmas season. The finishing on every project is simple and easy to follow, and will ensure your creations will be enjoyed for years to come. Each finishing technique can be applied to other projects, and colors and trends can be altered easily to fit your decor. Enjoy the designs and unique finishing ideas in this book and decorate your home with festive cross-stitch Christmas creations.

Contents

Introduction 1

Advent Stockings 3

Festive Friends 11

Chevron Christmas Trees 13

Falling Snowflakes 18

A Set of Santas 23

Nativity Silhouette Candle Wraps 26

Merry Christmas 31

Angel Tree Topper 35

Christmas Memories Frame 38

Elegant Ornament Trio 41

Christmas Motifs Explosion 44

Holiday Card Duo 47

Peppermint Gingerbread Cottage 50

How to Stitch 54

Special Thanks 56

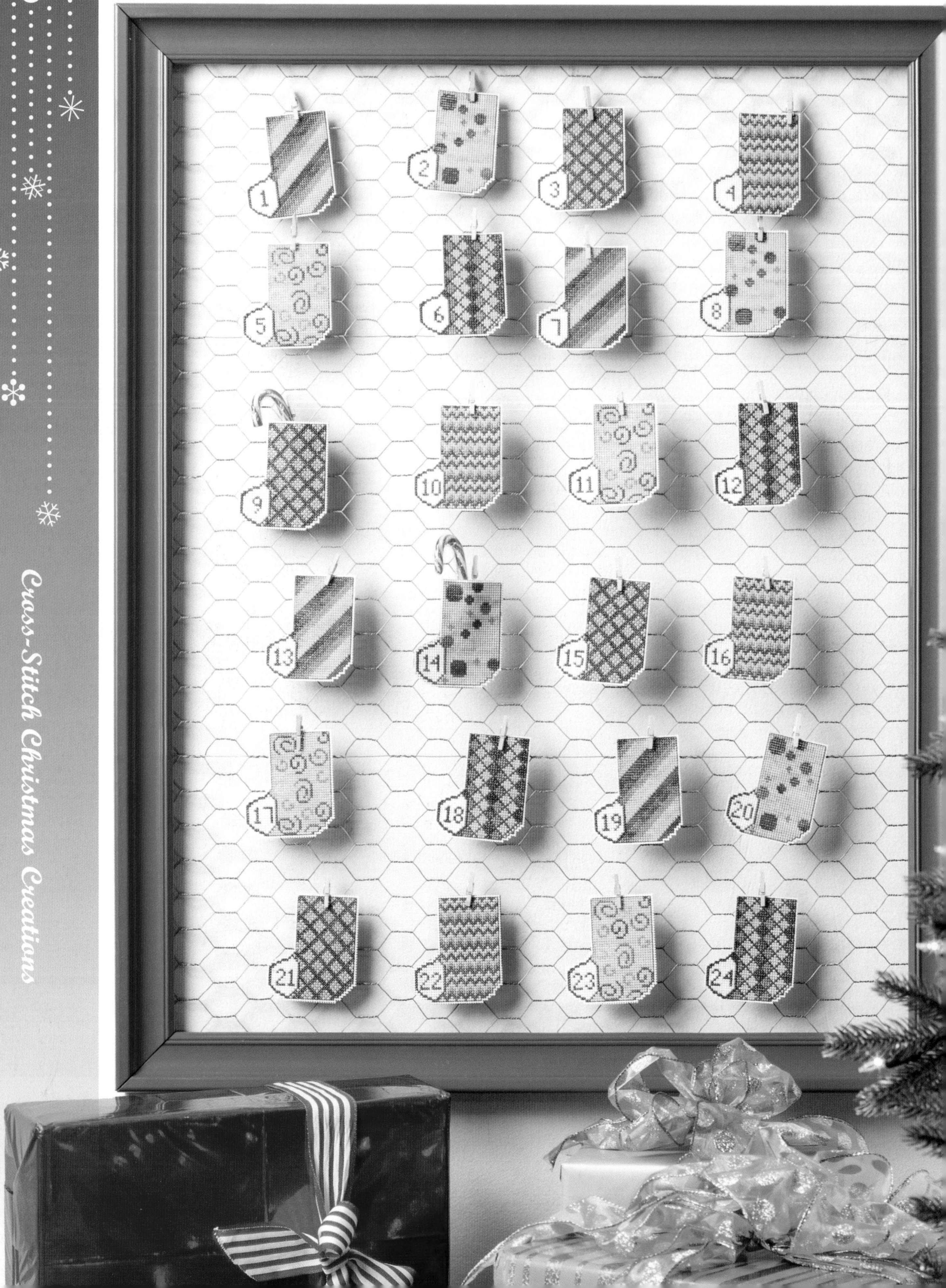
1
2
3
4
5
6
7
8
9
10
11
12
13
14
15
16
17
18
19
20
21
22
23
24

Advent Stockings

Designs by Christy Schmitz

Skill Level: Confident Beginner

Materials

- 24 (5" x 5") pieces 14-count white perforated paper from Wichelt Imports Inc.®*
- Four skeins each The Gentle Art Sampler Threads**
- Four skeins each The Gentle Art Simply Shaker Sampler Threads**
- Size 24 tapestry needle

*See Sources on page 56.
**Refer to color code.

The Gentle Art Sampler Threads
DMC® Alternatives Listed in Parentheses

■	0190 (936)	forest glade
╱	0920 (598)	tropical ocean**
@	0940 (3808)	island blue**
#	0390 (498)	buckeye scarlet*
○	0180 (471)	spring grass**

*Five skeins required.
**Six skeins required.

The Gentle Art Simply Shaker Sampler Threads
DMC® Alternatives Listed in Parentheses

•	7054 (blanc)	chalk
◑	7074 (469)	chives*

*Five skeins required.

Stitch Count: 42H x 36W each
Design Size: 3" x 2⅝" each

Instructions: Cross stitch over one square using two strands of floss.

Backstitch over one square using one strand 0190.

Finishing Materials & Instructions:
Four 8½" x 11" pieces coordinating cardstock
Two 8½" x 11" pieces coordinating scrapbook paper
22" x 28" frame
22" x 28" piece poultry fencing
Coordinating spray paint
Staple gun
24 small wooden clothespins
Acid-free glue stick
Advent fillers (small candies, slips of paper with winter activities)

Trim each stitched piece to one square from stitching on all sides. Using one trimmed piece as a template, cut 48 pieces of coordinating cardstock to same size. Glue one piece of cardstock to the back of each stitched piece; allow to adhere completely.

Glue a second piece of cardstock to the back of one pieced stocking, gluing only around the edges and bottom. Leave top open. Repeat for remaining stockings and cardstock pieces.

Spray-paint frame; allow to dry completely. Staple poultry fencing to back of frame. Insert advent fillers into stockings. Place stockings on poultry fencing and clip in place using small clothespins. ∽

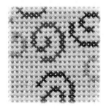

Stocking One

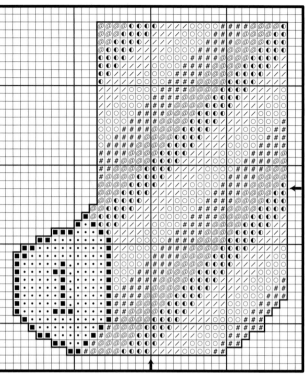

Stocking Two

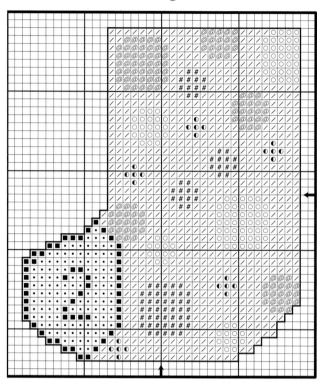

Stocking Three

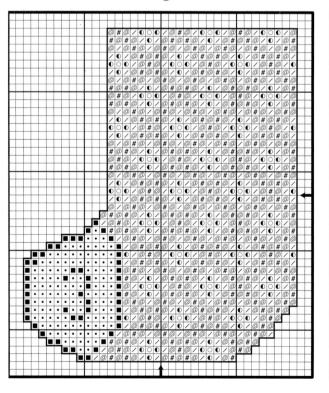

Stocking Four

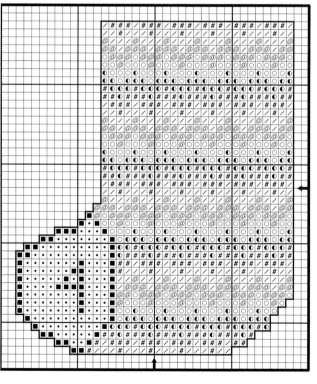

Stocking Five

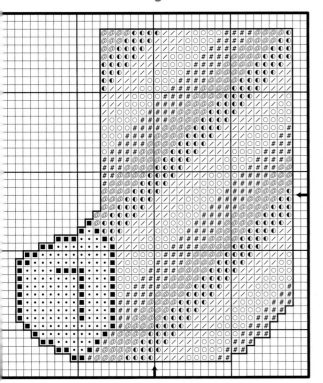

Stocking Six

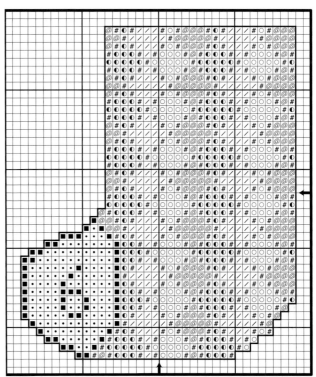

Stocking Seven

Stocking Eight

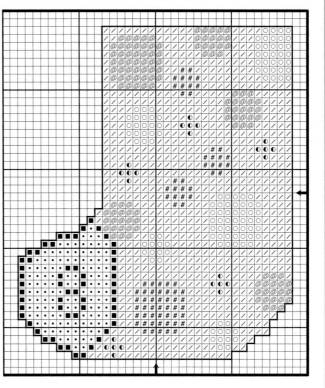

Stocking Nine

Stocking Ten

Stocking Eleven

Stocking Twelve

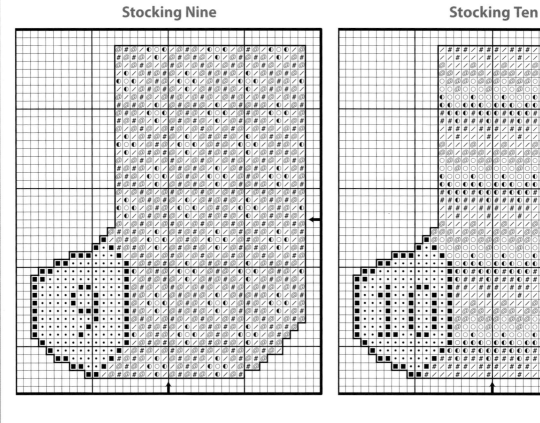
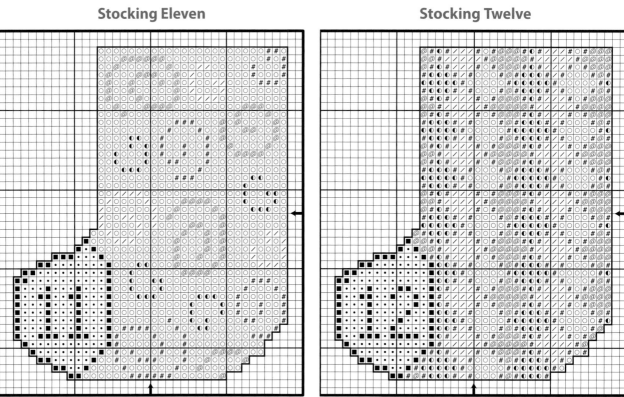

Stocking Thirteen

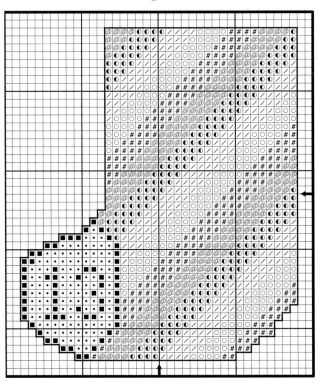

Stocking Fourteen

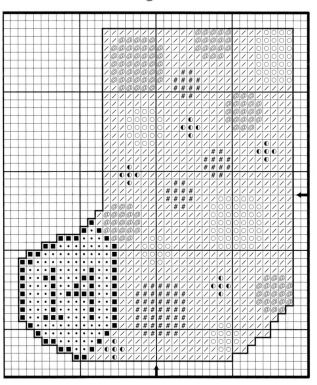

Stocking Fifteen

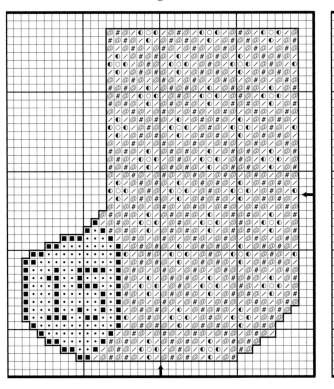

Stocking Sixteen

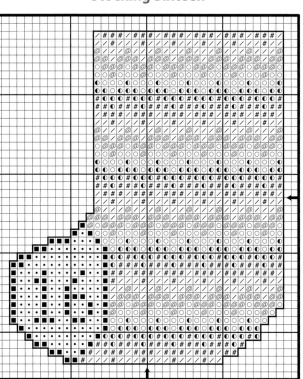

Stocking Seventeen

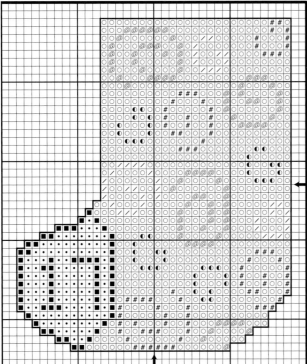

Stocking Eighteen

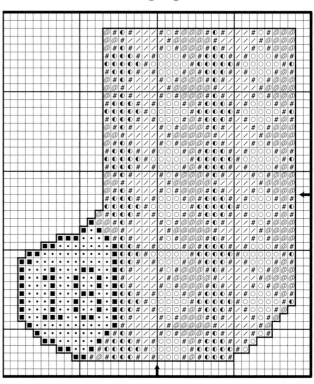

Stocking Nineteen

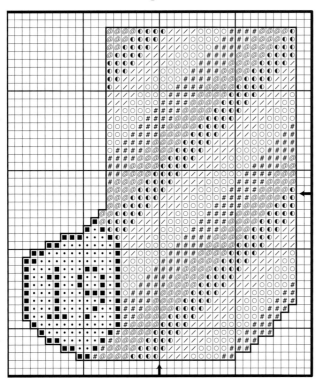

Stocking Twenty

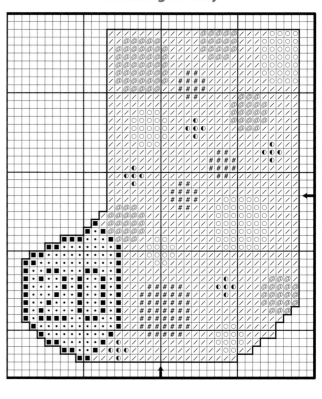

Stocking Twenty-One

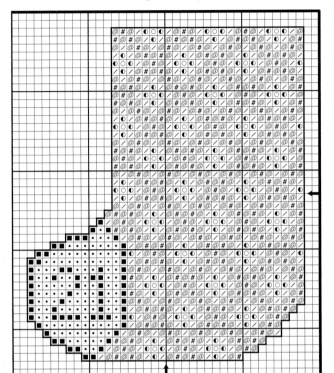

Stocking Twenty-Two

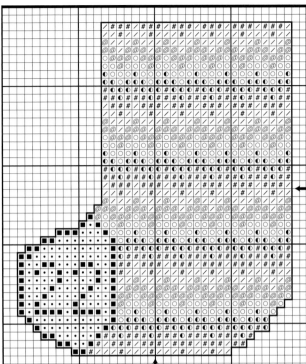

Stocking Twenty-Three

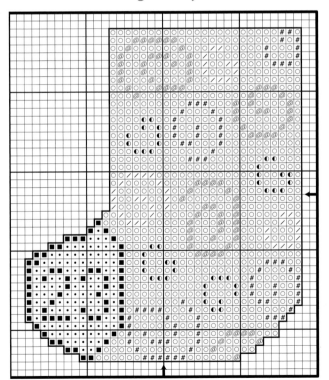

Stocking Twenty-Four

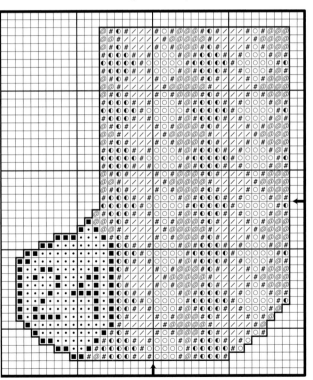

This whimsical trio of holiday friends will take center stage on any tree this holiday season. Bold, vibrant colors and adorable characters make these fun to stitch, and quick finishing instructions will have them hanging on your tree in no time.

Festive Friends

Designs by Sharon Pope

Skill Level: Beginner

Materials

- Three 6" x 5" pieces 14-count white perforated paper from Wichelt Imports Inc.*
- One skein each DMC® six-strand embroidery floss**
- Two spools Kreinik Very Fine Braid #4*
- Size 24 tapestry needle

*See Sources on page 56.
**Refer to color code.

DMC®

☆	350	coral, med.
♥	817	coral red, vy. dk.
♡	957	geranium, pl.
¶	956	geranium
a	209	lavender, dk.
◐	208	lavender, vy. dk.
ℓ	907	parrot green, lt.
G	906	parrot green, med.
~	519	sky blue
○	518	Wedgwood, lt.
@	517	Wedgwood, dk.
⊂	436	tan
з	435	brown, vy. lt.
✳	433	brown, med.
·	blanc	white
μ	415	pearl gray
z	414	steel gray, dk.
#	413	pewter gray, dk.
■	310	black
/	742	tangerine, lt.
4	741	tangerine, med.

Kreinik Very Fine Braid #4

ss	032	pearl

Stitch Count: 56H x 42W each
Design Size: 4" x 3" each

Instructions: Cross stitch over one square using two strands of floss.

Backstitch over one square using one strand 310.

Work French knot where ● appears using two strands of floss and wrapping floss around needle twice.

Work straight stitch (ss) using two strands of floss or one strand of very fine braid unless otherwise indicated.

Straight Stitch (ss) Instructions:
032 stars
956 scarf fringe on Penguin
906 scarf fringe on Snowman
433 Snowman's arms
208 scarf fringe on Reindeer

French Knot Instructions:
906 fringe on Penguin and Snowman scarves
208 fringe on Reindeer scarf

Finishing Materials & Instructions:
Three 4½" x 3½" pieces apple green cardstock
Three 10" lengths ¼"-wide white grosgrain ribbon
Glue stick

Trim each stitched design to one square from stitching on all sides. Center one stitched piece atop one piece of cardstock; glue in place. Glue ends of one length of ribbon to the back of layered stitched piece to make hanging loop. Repeat for remaining stitched pieces, cardstock and ribbon.

Penguin

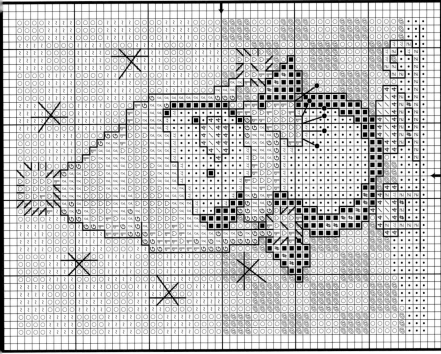

Reindeer

Top

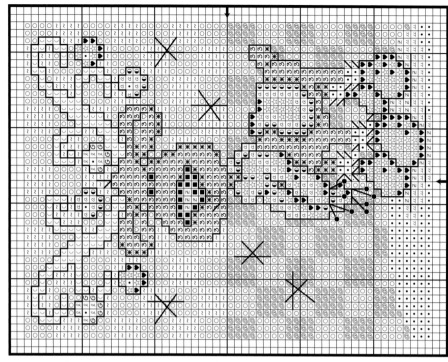

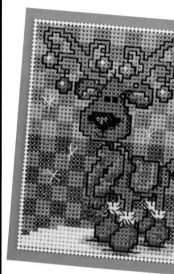

Snowman

Top

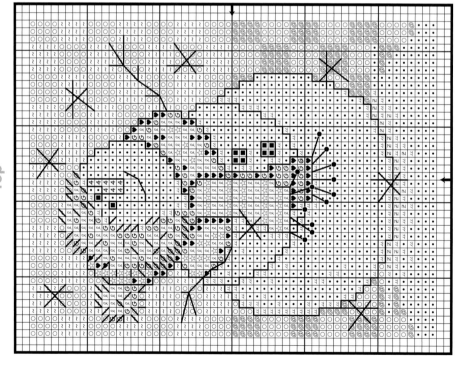

Chevron Christmas Trees

Designs by Patti Connor of SamSarah Design Studio

This trio of chevron-patterned trees is sure to elicit plenty of oohs and aahs from holiday guests. Simple cross stitch and easy-to-follow finishing instructions will have these gracing your holiday mantel in no time.

Skill Level: Beginner

Materials

- Three 9" x 12" pieces 14-count white perforated paper from Wichelt Imports Inc.*
- Three skeins each Weeks Dye Works™ Hand Over Dyed Floss**
- Size 24 tapestry needle

See Where to Find It on page 56.
**Refer to color code.*

**Weeks Dye Works™
Hand Over Dyed Floss**

DMC® Alternatives Listed in Parentheses

@	2120 (518)	capri*
♥	2258 (347)	Aztec red*
○	1150 (646)	Spanish moss
·	1092 (3865)	grits**

Four skeins required.
**Seven skeins required.*

Stitch Count:
Blue Tree: 111H x 84W
Red Tree: 111H x 70W
Gray Tree: 78H x 78W

Design Size:
Blue Tree: 8" x 6"
Red Tree: 8" x 5"
Gray Tree: 5⅝" x 5⅝"

Instructions: Cross stitch over one square using two strands of floss.

Note: *Red lines are for finishing and should not be backstitched.*

Finishing Materials & Instructions:
Three 8½" x 11" pieces coordinating scrapbook paper
Three 1½"-diameter x ½"-thick wooden tread wheels with ¼"-diameter center hole
Three ¼"-diameter wooden dowels in the following lengths: 5½", 6" and 8"
Silver spray paint
Craft glue
Small paintbrush
Paper clips or binder clips

Trim stitched design along red line on chart, including tab on side. Use trimmed Blue Tree stitched piece to cut coordinating scrapbook paper to same size, keeping side edges equal but removing a margin equal to one row of stitching to the pointed edges so scrapbook paper is slightly smaller than the Tree. Repeat for Red and Gray trees and scrapbook papers.

Gently roll Blue Tree cut-out scrapbook paper to form a cone and fold back tabs at edge of stitching, especially at the top. You may need to trim top edges of the tab diagonally to help top of cone come to a point. Paint white glue on the right side of tab, roll back into a cone and secure tab to underside of opposite cut edge. Hold in place with paper clips or binder clips until glue sets. Repeat process for remaining cut-out scrapbook papers and remaining stitched pieces. Allow to dry completely.

Stack Blue Tree stitched piece atop large scrapbook paper cone and test fit; if necessary, trim scrapbook paper cone to fit. Carefully paint craft glue on inside of stitched piece from pointed edge to ½" from pointed edge. Place over scrapbook paper and hold in place until glue sets. Repeat for Red and Gray Trees scrapbook paper cutouts and stitched pieces. Allow to dry completely.

Spray-paint wheels and dowels and allow to dry completely. Insert dowels into wheels and glue in place if necessary to secure. Place Blue Tree over 8"-tall dowel, Red Tree over 6" dowel and Gray Tree over 5½" dowel. ✿

Blue Tree

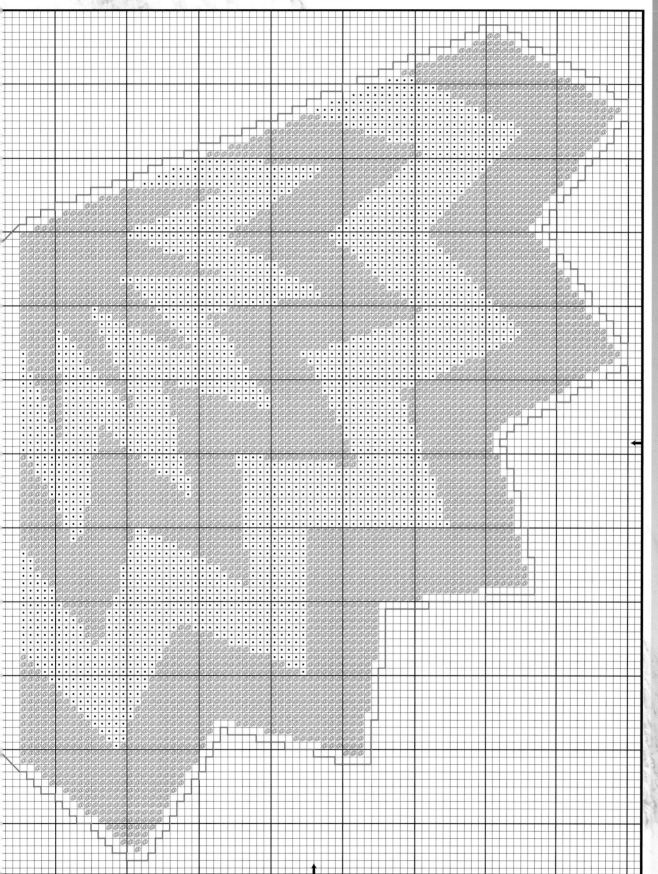

Red Tree

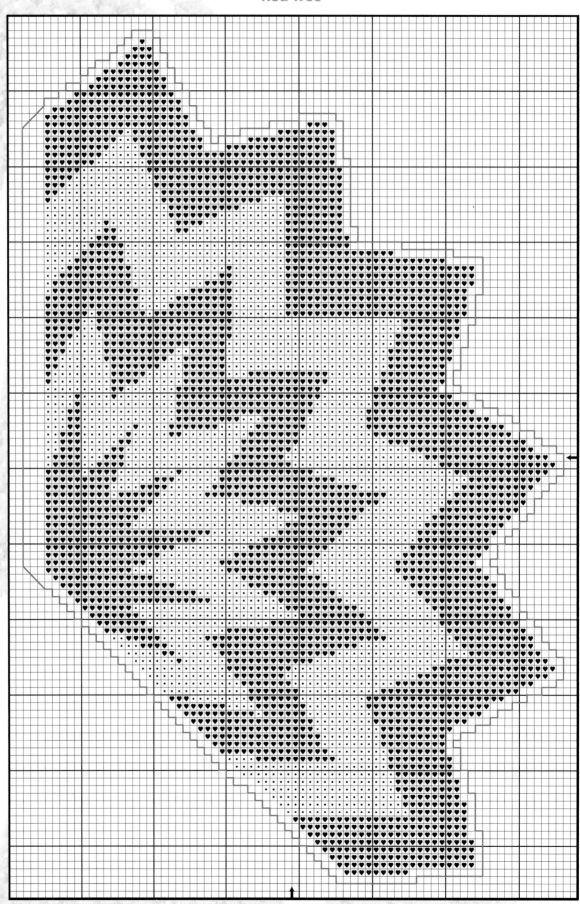

Gray Tree

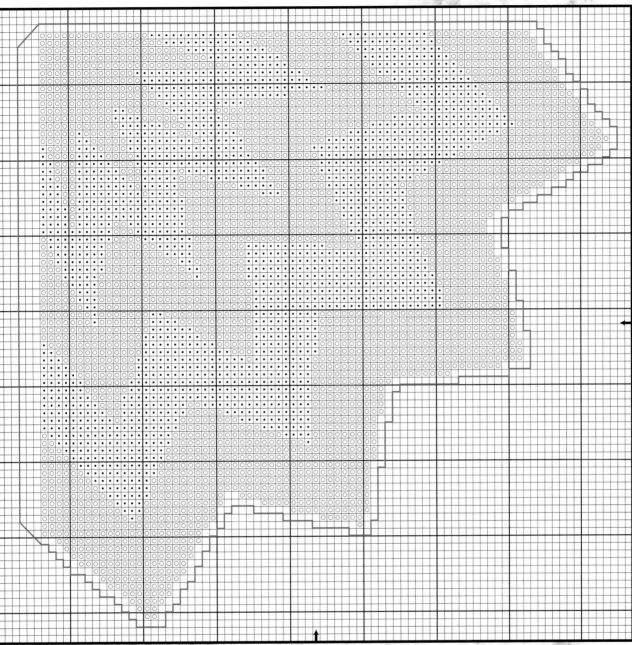

Falling Snowflakes

Designs by Sharon Pope

Christmas and the holiday season are synonymous with falling snow. The glittery one-of-a-kind snowflakes fall gracefully with a fleeting beauty. You can capture this beauty with this set of six snowflake designs.

Snowflake One

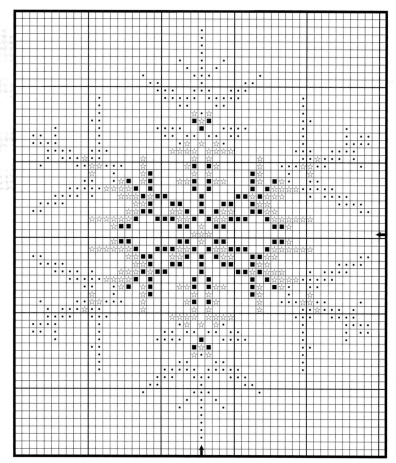

Skill Level: Beginner

Materials

- Six 6" x 6" pieces 14-count white perforated paper from Wichelt Imports Inc.*
- One skein each DMC® six-strand embroidery floss**
- Two spools Kreinik Blending Filament*
- Size 24 tapestry needle

*See Sources on page 56.
**Refer to color code.

DMC®

- 3756   baby blue, ul. vy. lt.
- 211   lavender, lt.
- 032 KBF   pearl
- 3841   baby blue, pl.
- 210   lavender, med.
- 032 KBF   pearl
- 3755   baby blue
- 209   lavender, dk.
- 032 KBF   pearl

Kreinik Blending Filament
032   pearl

Stitch Count:
Snowflake One: 55H x 47W
Snowflake Two: 56H x 53W
Snowflake Three: 53H x 45W
Snowflake Four: 51H x 51W
Snowflake Five: 55H x 53W
Snowflake Six: 53H x 51W

Design Size:
Snowflake One: 4" x 3⅜"
Snowflake Two: 4" x 3⅞"
Snowflake Three: 3⅞" x 3¼"
Snowflake Four: 3⅔" x 3⅔"
Snowflake Five: 4" x 3⅞"
Snowflake Six: 3⅞" x 3⅔"

Instructions: Cross stitch over one square using one strand of each floss and one strand of blending filament.

Snowflake Two

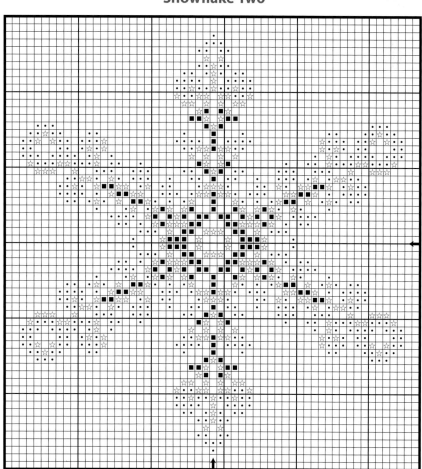

Snowflake Three

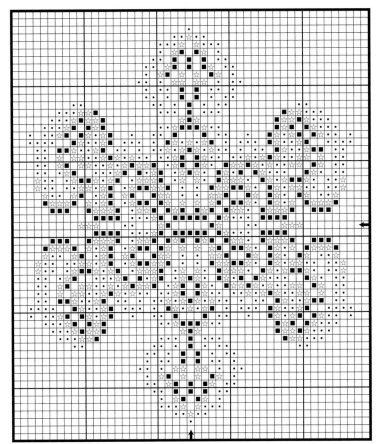

Finishing Materials & Instructions:

Six 5" x 5" pieces coordinating
   scrapbook paper
13" x 13" frame
Silver spray paint
Clear fishing line
Glue stick
Hot-glue gun

Spray-paint frame; allow
to dry completely.

Trim each stitched piece
to one square from stitching
on all sides. Using trimmed
stitched pieces as templates,
cut coordinating scrapbook
paper to same size; glue
same-size paper to back of
each stitched piece.

Cut six pieces of fishing
line to varying lengths to fit
into frame. Attach one end of
each length to one stitched
piece. Position snowflakes as
desired and attach other end
of fishing line to back of frame
using hot glue. ✍

Snowflake Four

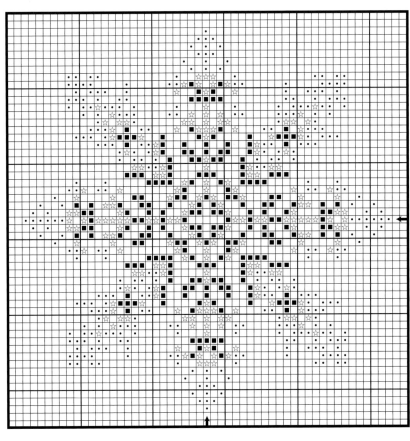

Snowflake Five

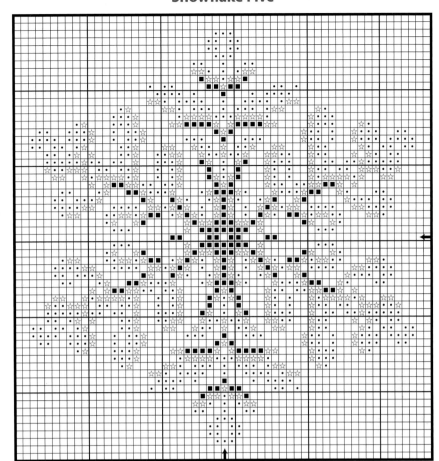

Snowflake Six

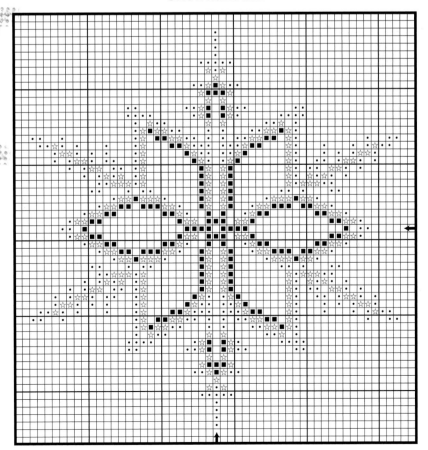

A Set of Santas

Designs by Donna V. Giampa
of The Vermillion Stitchery

Few faces are more iconic in the holiday season than Santa Claus, and this charming set will have your tabletop decked out with the jolliest elf.

Skill Level: Intermediate

Materials

- Five 5" x 5" pieces 14-count white perforated paper from Wichelt Imports Inc.*
- One skein each DMC® six-strand embroidery floss**
- One skein each DMC® Metallic Pearl Cotton #5**
- Size 24 tapestry needle

*See Sources on page 56.
**Refer to color code.

DMC®

■	898	coffee brown, vy. dk.
4	434	brown, lt.
b	436	tan
∞	738	tan, vy. lt.
X	642	beige gray, dk.
◇	644	beige gray, med.
~	822	beige gray, lt.
●	300	mahogany, vy. dk.
8	780	topaz, ul. vy. dk.
☆	782	topaz, dk.
C	676	old gold, lt.
−	677	old gold, vy. lt.
#	839	beige brown, dk.
⊗	840	beige brown, med.
/	762	pearl gray, vy. lt.
★	890	pistachio green, ul. dk.
G	501	blue green, dk.
∷	319	pistachio green, vy. dk.
$	320	pistachio green, med.
3	367	pistachio green, dk.
△	368	pistachio green, lt.
++	369	pistachio green, vy. lt.
¶	3347	yellow green, med.
♥	814	garnet, dk.
@	498	red, dk.
«	349	coral, dk.
○	321	red

μ	3778	terra cotta, lt.
κ	758	terra cotta, vy. lt.
ℓ	754	peach, lt.
+	948	peach, vy. lt.
♡	760	salmon
α	761	salmon, lt.
£	311	navy blue, med.
◐	322	baby blue, vy. dk.
z	775	baby blue, vy. lt.
·	blanc	white
bs	413	pewter gray, dk.
bs	938	coffee brown, ul. dk.

DMC® Metallic Pearl Cotton #5

✱	5282	gold, lt.

Stitch Count: 43H x 43W each
Design Size: 3⅛" x 3⅛" each

Instructions: Cross stitch over one square using two strands of floss.
    Backstitch over one square using one strand of floss.

Backstitch (bs) Instructions
Holly Santa

890	holly leaves
413	hair, mustache and beard
938	remainder of backstitch

Holly Santa

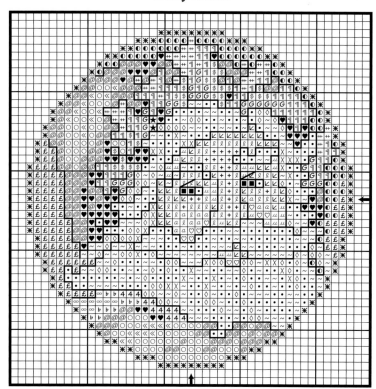

Red Coat Santa
413   hair and beard
938   remainder of backstitch

Star Santa
938   red part of hat, eyes
300   nose, stars
413   remainder of backstitch

Jingle Bell Santa
413   hair, eyebrows, beard
890   green holly
938   remainder of backstitch

Toy Bag Santa
311   glove
413   hair, mustache and beard
938   remainder of backstitch

Finishing Materials & Instructions:
Four round acrylic coasters (#3292) from Yarn Tree*
4" x 4" x 4" papier-mâché box
Five 5" x 5" pieces white cardstock
Glue stick
18" length ⅝"-wide red-and-white ribbon
*See Sources on page 56.

Trim stitched pieces to one square from stitching on all sides. Using trimmed pieces as templates, cut cardstock to same size. Glue a cardstock piece to the back of each stitched piece. Following manufacturer's instructions, insert one backed stitched piece into each coaster.

Center and glue remaining backed stitched piece to top of papier-mâché box. Glue ribbon around middle of box, centering and folding under raw ends of ribbon. ✍

Red Coat Santa

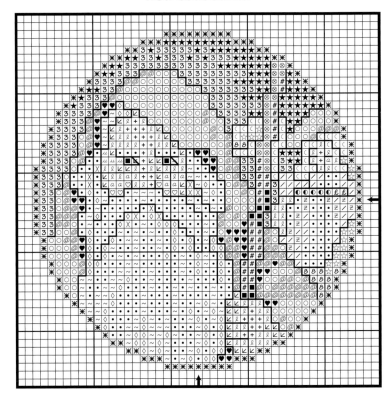

Star Santa

Jingle Bell Santa

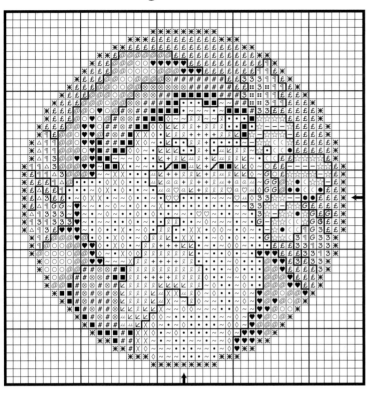

Toy Bag Santa

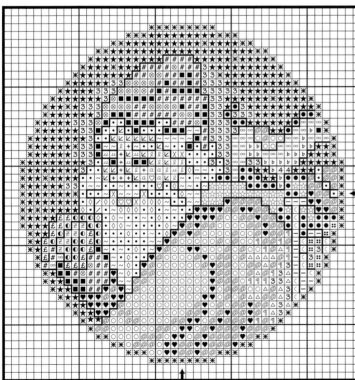

Nativity Silhouette Candle Wraps

Designs by Sharon Pope

The warm glow of candlelight coordinates beautifully with these silhouette designs. Stitched entirely in a single floss color, the design exudes timeless elegance.

Skill Level: Beginner

Materials

- Three 9" x 12" pieces 14-count antique brown perforated paper from Wichelt Imports Inc.*
- Three skeins DMC® six-strand embroidery floss**
- Size 24 tapestry needle
  See Sources on page 56.
  **Refer to color code.*

DMC®

■ 310   black

Stitch Count

Holy Family: 84H x 126W
Shepherds: 66H x 126W
Magi: 66H x 126W

Design Size
Holy Family: 6" x 9"
Shepherds: 4¾" x 9"
Magi: 4¾" x 9"

Instructions: Cross stitch over one square using two strands of floss.

Backstitch over one square using two strands 310.

Work French knot where ● appears using two strands 310.

Work straight stitch using two strands 310.

Finishing Materials & Instructions:
Two 8" x 4" glass candleholders
One 8" x 7" glass candleholder
18" length 1½"-wide black burlap ribbon
Craft glue or permanent glue dots

Trim each stitched piece to seven squares from stitching on bottom. Trim top of each stitched design to make trimmed piece 7" high; do not trim sides. Position Holy Family stitched piece around 7" candleholder and determine length of ribbon to connect ends around candleholder. Cut ribbon to desired length. Glue one end of ribbon to back of right-hand side of stitched piece. Position stitched piece around candleholder and glue remaining end of ribbon to left-hand side of stitched piece, making sure design fits candleholder snugly. Repeat for Shepherds and Magi with 4" candleholders. ✑

Skill Level: Beginner

Materials

- Three 9" x 12" pieces 14-count antique brown perforated paper from Wichelt Imports Inc.*
- Three skeins DMC® six-strand embroidery floss**
- Size 24 tapestry needle
  See Sources on page 56.
  **Refer to color code.*

DMC®

■ 310   black

Stitch Count

Holy Family: 84H x 126W
Shepherds: 66H x 126W
Magi: 66H x 126W

Design Size
Holy Family: 6" x 9"
Shepherds: 4¾" x 9"
Magi: 4¾" x 9"

Instructions: Cross stitch over one square using two strands of floss.

Backstitch over one square using two strands 310.

Work French knot where ● appears using two strands 310.

Work straight stitch using two strands 310.

Finishing Materials & Instructions:
Two 8" x 4" glass candleholders
One 8" x 7" glass candleholder
18" length 1½"-wide black burlap ribbon
Craft glue or permanent glue dots

Trim each stitched piece to seven squares from stitching on bottom. Trim top of each stitched design to make trimmed piece 7" high; do not trim sides. Position Holy Family stitched piece around 7" candleholder and determine length of ribbon to connect ends around candleholder. Cut ribbon to desired length. Glue one end of ribbon to back of right-hand side of stitched piece. Position stitched piece around candleholder and glue remaining end of ribbon to left-hand side of stitched piece, making sure design fits candleholder snugly. Repeat for Shepherds and Magi with 4" candleholders.

Cross-Stitch Christmas Creations

Holy Family

Top

Top

Cross-Stitch Christmas Creations

Magi

Top

Magi

Merry Christmas

Design by Elizabeth Spurlock

Reminiscent of a Victorian sentiment or greeting card, this design combines timeless elegance and bold jewel tones.

Cross-Stitch Christmas Creations

Skill Level: Beginner

Materials

· 8" x 13" piece 14-count white perforated paper from Wichelt Imports Inc.*
· One skein each DMC® six-strand embroidery floss**
· One skein DMC® Color Variations six-strand embroidery floss**
· One skein each DMC® Light Effects metallic floss**
· Size 24 tapestry needle
· Professionally framed*

*See Sources on page 56.
**Refer to color code.

DMC®

■	154	grape, vy. dk.
X	318	steel gray, lt.
★	319	pistachio green, vy. dk.
∕	367	pistachio green, dk.
#	797	royal blue
○	798	Delft blue, dk.
κ	820	royal blue, vy. dk.
◑	991	aquamarine, dk.
~	992	aquamarine, lt.
♥	3685	mauve, vy. dk.
ℓ	3687	mauve
@	3803	mauve, dk.
$	3814	aquamarine
¶	3834	grape, dk.
μ	3835	grape, med.

DMC® Color Variations

●	4210	radiant ruby

DMC® Light Effects

·	E168	silver
☆	E3852	gold, dk.

Stitch Count: 56H x 32W
Design Size: 4" x 2⅓"

Instructions: Cross stitch over one square using two strands of floss.

Backstitch over one square using one strand of floss.

Backstitch (bs) Instructions:

820	blue and silver ornament
154	purple and gold ornament
3685	mauve and silver ornament
E3852	green and gold ornament ༺

Top

Angel Tree Topper

Design by Angela Pullen Atherton of Pullen Designs

Grace the top of your holiday focal point with this elegant angelic tree topper. Dressed in rich hues of greens and reds, the angel topper is also a quick finish with the use of a single sheet of acetate.

Skill Level: Beginner

Materials

- 9" x 12" piece 14-count white perforated paper from Wichelt Imports Inc.*
- One skein each DMC® six-strand embroidery floss**
- One skein each DMC® Light Effects metallic floss**
- Size 24 tapestry needle

*See Sources on page 56.
**Refer to color code.

DMC®

£	760	salmon
/	948	peach, vy. lt.
ℓ	754	peach, lt.
♡	758	terra cotta, vy. lt.
•	blanc	white
~	3072	beaver gray, vy. lt.
X	648	beaver gray, lt.
+	646	beaver gray, dk.
△	676	old gold, lt.
¥	729	old gold, med.
::	680	old gold, dk.
μ	3801	melon, vy. dk.
@	498	red, dk.
◐	815	garnet, med.
★	814	garnet, dk.
(	368	pistachio green, lt.
○	320	pistachio green, med.
#	367	pistachio green, dk.
■	319	pistachio green, vy. dk.
☆	989	forest green
$	987	forest green, dk.
bs	420	hazelnut brown, dk.
bs	645	beaver gray, vy. dk.
bs	869	hazelnut brown, vy. dk.
bs	986	forest green, vy. dk.

DMC® Light Effects

◇	E3821	gold, lt.
✳	E3852	gold, dk.
⬏	E436	golden oak

Stitch Count: 139H x 88W
Design Size: 10" x 6⅓"

Instructions: Cross stitch over one square using two strands of floss.

Backstitch over one square using one strand of floss.

Work French knot where
● appears using two strands
E3852.

Backstitch (bs) Instructions:

420	facial features; outline of face, hair and hands; neckline
869	red stole, halo
645	wings, bottom of skirt
986	green dress, including bodice

Finishing Materials & Instructions:
6" x 15" piece acetate
8½" x 11" piece coordinating cardstock
Glue stick
Permanent glue dots

Trim stitched piece to one square from stitching on all sides. Using trimmed piece as a template, cut coordinating cardstock to same size. Glue cut-out cardstock to the back of stitched design. Roll acetate into a cone shape, checking to make sure cone fits on back of stitched piece; glue cone edges using glue stick. Position cone on back of stitched piece with large open end at bottom; adhere cone to stitched piece using permanent glue dots. ✍

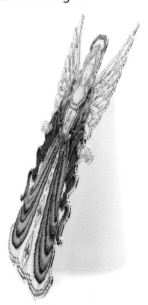

Cross-Stitch Christmas Creations

Angel Tree Topper

Top

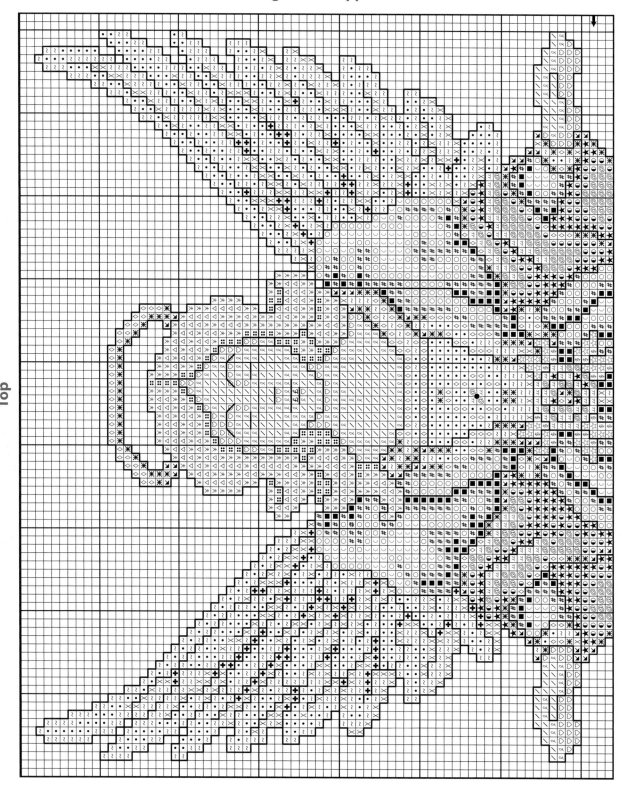

Shaded portion indicates overlap from previous page.

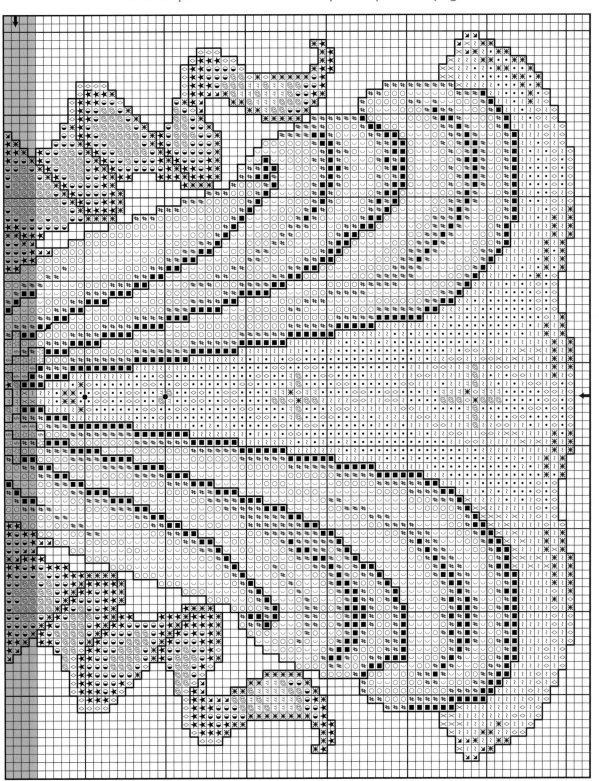

Top

Christmas Memories Frame

Design by Breanne Jackson

Frame your favorite photo in a zigzag stripe of red, white and green in this adorable frame design. Variegated flosses lend subtle movement to the repeating pattern, making this design one that you will be excited to display every holiday.

Skill Level: Beginner

Materials

· 9" x 11" piece 14-count white perforated paper from Wichelt Imports Inc.*
· Two skeins each Weeks Dye Works™ Hand Over Dyed Floss**

· Size 24 tapestry needle
· Prefinished 5" x 7" black frame*

*See Sources on page 56.
**Refer to color code.

**Weeks Dye Works™
Hand Over Dyed Floss**
DMC® Alternatives Listed in Parentheses

♥ 2259 (498)   cayenne
☆ 2168 (987)   monkey grass
· 1091 (blanc) whitewash

Stitch Count: 70H x 98W
Design Size: 5" x 7"

Instructions: Cross stitch over one square using two strands of floss. ➷

Christmas Memories Frame

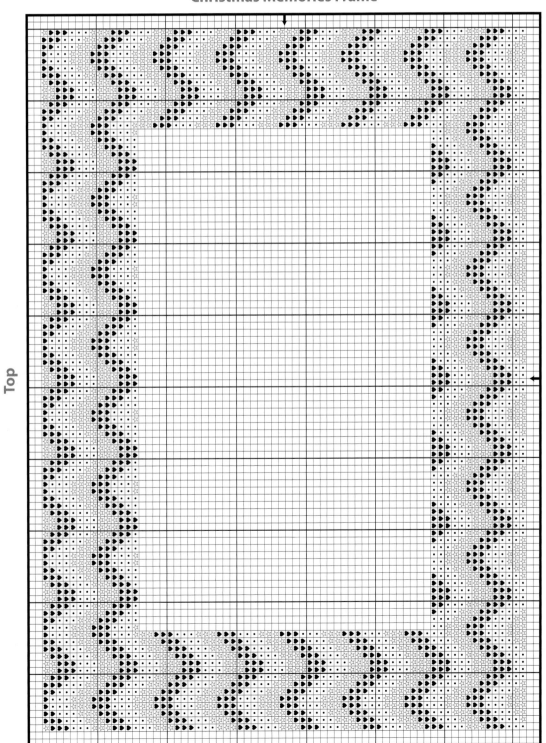

Top

Elegant Ornament Trio

Designs by Marie Barber

Add sparkle and elegance to your Christmas tree with this trio of ornaments. Stitched in trendy and timeless turquoise, red and black, the ornaments will be treasured holiday additions for years to come.

Skill Level: Beginner

Materials

· Three 8" x 7" pieces 14-count metallic silver perforated paper from Wichelt Imports Inc.*
· One skein DMC® six-strand embroidery floss**
· One spool each Kreinik Very Fine Braid #4**
· Size 24 tapestry needle

*See Sources on page 56.
**Refer to color code.

Ornament A

DMC®

ℓ	3849	teal green, lt.
○	666	red, bt.
■	310	black

Kreinik Very Fine Braid #4

◑	085	peacock
·	032	pearl
@	029	turquoise
☆	212	golden sand
bs	005	black

Ornament B

DMC®

~	3890	bright turquoise, vy. lt.
○ ⌐	3846	bright turquoise, lt.
⌐	3810	turquoise, dk.
@	3809	turquoise, vy. dk.
★	3808	turquoise, ul. vy. dk.
♩	3847	teal green, dk.
Fk	310	black

Kreinik Very Fine Braid #4

■	005	black
·	032	pearl
⊔	3228	topaz
╱	5760	marshmallow
bs	085	peacock

Ornament C

DMC®

■	310	black
╱	3811	turquoise, vy. lt.
@	3808	turquoise, ul. vy. dk.
○	3849	teal green, lt.
Fk	3890	bright turquoise, vy. lt.

Kreinik Very Fine Braid #4

☆	029	turquoise
◑	005	black
♩	028	citron
·	5760	marshmallow

Stitch Count: 56H x 32W each
Design Size: 4" x 2⅓" each

Instructions: Cross stitch over one square using two strands of floss or one strand of very fine braid.

Backstitch over one square using one strand of floss or very fine braid.

Work French knot (Fk) where ● appears using one strand of floss.

Backstitch (bs) Instructions:

005	Ornament A, horizontal lines on Ornament B, Ornament C
085	diagonal detail lines on Ornament B

French Knot (Fk) Instructions:

666	Ornament A
310	Ornament B
3890	Ornament C

Finishing Materials & Instructions:
8" x 11" piece silver cardstock
Three 9" lengths ⅛"-wide black satin ribbon
Craft glue

Trim stitched design to one square from stitching on all sides. Using trimmed piece as a template, cut cardstock to same size. Glue cardstock to reverse side of stitched piece. Attach hanging loop of black ribbon on back of ornament. ✍

Ornament A

Top

Ornament B

Top

Ornament C

Top

Christmas Motifs Explosion

Designs by Breanne Jackson

Small, quick-to-stitch motifs are perfect for all of your holiday decorating needs. From gift tags to magnets, treat toppers and cookie-mix jars, these nine tiny treasures will bring a smile to the face of every recipient. Simple finishing instructions explain each technique, and all of them can be finished as ornaments for a tiny desktop tree.

Skill Level: Beginner

Materials

· Nine 4" x 4" pieces 14-count white perforated paper from Wichelt Imports Inc.*
· One skein each DMC® six-strand embroidery floss**
· Size 24 tapestry needle

*See Sources on page 56.
**Refer to color code.

	DMC®	
·	blanc	white
µ	3770	tawny, vy. lt.
♥	321	red
■	310	black
£	945	tawny
★	905	parrot green, dk.
◐	435	brown, vy. lt.
@	3803	mauve, dk.
○	169	pewter, lt.
¶	598	turquoise, lt.
✶	666	red, bt.
△	702	kelly green

Stitch Count:
Elf: 24H x 19W
Gift: 23H x 18W
Snowman: 25H x 18W
Candy Cane: 24H x 15W
Santa: 25H x 21W
Striped Ornament: 24H x 15W
Purple Ornament: 26H x 17W
Mitten: 24H x 21W
Gingerbread Girl: 24H x 19W

Design Size:
Elf: 1¾" x 1⅜"
Gift: 1⅔" x 1⅓"
Snowman: 1⅞" x 1⅓"
Candy Cane: 1¾" x 1⅛"
Santa: 1½" x 1⅝"
Striped Ornament: 1⅞" x 1⅛"
Purple Ornament: 1⅞" x 1¼"
Mitten: 1¾" x 1½"
Gingerbread Girl: 1¾" x 1⅜"

Instructions: Cross stitch over one square using two strands of floss.

Backstitch over one square using one strand of floss.

Backstitch Instructions:
945 elf face
310 remainder of backstitch

Finishing Materials & Instructions:
Coordinating cardstock
Glue stick
Ruler
Lollipop sticks
Self-adhesive ½"-diameter magnet cirles
Ribbon

Trim each stitched design to one square beyond stitching on all sides.

Gift Tag—Cut one 6" x 3" piece of coordinating cardstock. Referring to photo, trim corners from one end of tag. Attach stitched design to end of tag as show. Punch hole through left end of tag. Loop ribbon through hole; trim ends.

Elf

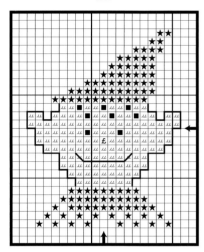

Gift

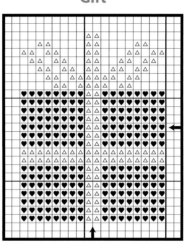

Snowman

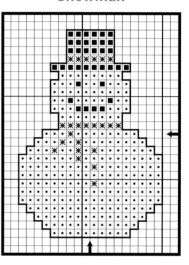

Candy Bag Topper—Cut one 6" x 4¼" piece of coordinating cardstock. Score and fold cardstock in half lengthwise. Cut one 5½" x 1⅞" piece of coordinating cardstock. Glue on front of Topper, centering. Attach stitched designs to ends of Topper.

Cupcake Topper—Cut one 2⅜"-diameter circle from coordinating cardstock. Center stitched motif in center of circle and glue in place. Glue lollipop stick on back.

Magnets—Glue trimmed stitched pieces to coordinating cardstock and trim. Attach magnet to back of cardstock.

Cookie Mix—Cut one 2⅜"-diameter circle from coordinating cardstock. Glue piece on center of length of ribbon; wrap ribbon around jar and secure. ✍

Candy Cane

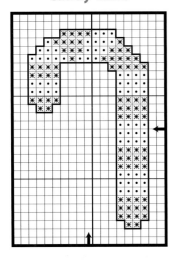

Santa

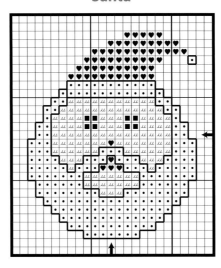

Purple Ornament

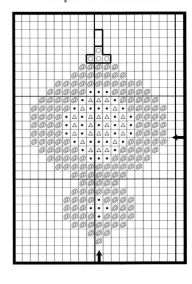

Striped Ornament

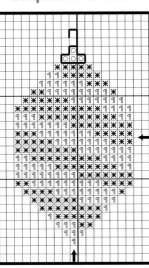

Mitten

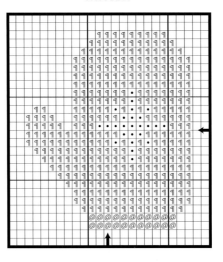

Gingerbread Girl

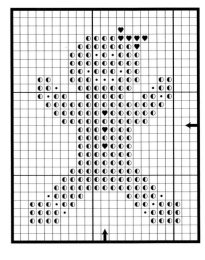

Cross-Stitch Christmas Creations

Holiday Card Duo

Designs by Donna V. Giampa
of The Vermillion Stitchery

Add a special element to your holiday cards with these two elegant designs. A festive, vivid poinsettia and the quintessential partridge in a pear tree pair with easy-to-following finishing instructions for cards that will amaze your friends and family.

Skill Level: Intermediate

Materials

- Two 6" x 6" pieces 14-count white perforated paper from Wichelt Imports Inc.*
- One skein each DMC® six-strand embroidery floss**
- Size 24 tapestry needle

*See Sources on page 56.
**Refer to color code.

DMC®

♥	498	red, dk.
◑	321	red
@	666	red, bt.
/	3801	melon, vy. dk.
○	3705	melon, dk.
ɑ	3706	melon, med.
⊾	895	hunter green, vy. dk.
+	319	pistachio green, vy. dk.
3	367	pistachio green, dk.
☆	320	pistachio green, med.
z	368	pistachio green, lt.
8	904	parrot green, vy. dk.
$	905	parrot green, dk.
μ	906	parrot green, med.
–	907	parrot green, lt.
#	782	topaz, dk.
::	3852	straw, vy. dk.
♡	3820	straw, dk.
//	3821	straw
ℓ	3822	straw, lt.
¥	725	topaz, med. lt.
C	727	topaz, vy. lt.
■	310	black
✳	3799	pewter gray, vy. dk.
G	413	pewter gray, dk.
⊗	414	steel gray, dk.
%	318	steel gray, lt.
△	415	pearl gray
~	762	pearl gray, vy. lt.
·	blanc	white
●	938	coffee brown, ul. dk.
★	434	brown, lt.
+	435	brown, vy. lt.
X	947	burnt orange
bs	902	garnet, vy. dk.

Stitch Count:

Poinsettia: 52H x 52W
Partridge: 45H x 45W

Design Size:

Poinsettia: 3¾" x 3¾"
Partridge: 3¼" x 3¼"

Instructions: Cross stitch over one square using two strands of floss.

Backstitch (bs) over one square using one strand of floss.

Backstitch (bs) Instructions:

902	Poinsettia petals
895	Poinsettia leaves
498	red ribbon and bows on Partridge
319	green leaves on Partridge
3799	Partridge
434	pears
947	beak and eye

Finishing Materials & Instructions:

Two 5½" x 11" pieces red cardstock
Two 5" x 5" pieces coordinating scrapbook paper
6" x 6" piece dark green embossed cardstock
5" x 5" piece apple green embossed cardstock
Spellbinders™ die templates: Grand Circles #LF-114, Standard Circles LG #S4-114*

Cross-Stitch Christmas Creations

Die-cutting machine
Glue stick
Bone folder
Metallic marker
See Sources on page 56.

tip

Don't have a die-cutting machine? No problem! Just use our dimensions and a compass or even the bottom of a glass to create the circular shapes.

Trim each stitched piece to measure 5" x 5" using sharp embroidery scissors. Using trimmed stitched pieces as templates, cut two pieces of coordinating scrapbook paper to same size; glue to back of stitched piece. Set aside.

Fold one 5½" x 11" piece of red cardstock in half to make a 5½" x 5½" card and press along fold using a bone folder. Repeat for remaining piece of red cardstock.

Poinsettia—Using smallest (4¼") Grand Circles die template, center and die-cut a circle in front of one red card. Using third-smallest (5¼") die, die-cut a circle from apple green cardstock; center 4¼"-diameter Grand Circles die template atop circle and die-cut circle from center to create a "ring" of cardstock. Align ring over opening in red card and glue in place. Position stitched design inside front of red card with design centered in circle opening. Glue in place around edges. Embellish card front with metallic marker as desired.

Poinsettia

Partridge—Using largest (3¾") Standard Circles LG die template, center and die-cut a hole in front of one red card. Using second-smallest (4¾") die from Grand Circles, die-cut a circle from dark green cardstock; center 3¾"-diameter die atop circle and die-cut out center to create a "ring" of cardstock. Align ring over circle opening in red card and glue in place. Position stitched piece inside front of red card with design centered in circle opening. Glue in place around edges. Embellish card front with metallic marker as desired. ☙

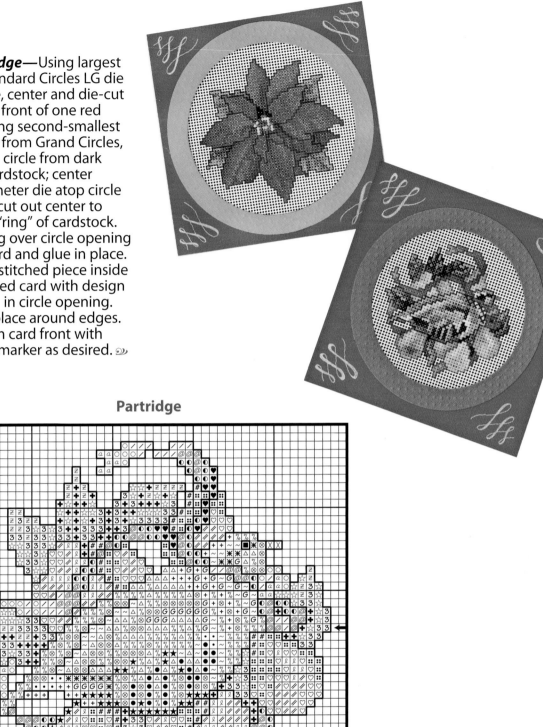

Partridge

Peppermint Gingerbread Cottage

Design by Christy Schmitz

Stitch a delightful 3-D gingerbread house that will dazzle and amaze for years to come. Simple cross stitches and easy-to-follow finishing instructions will have this piece resting in a place of honor on your tabletop in no time.

Skill Level: Confident Beginner

Materials

- Three 5" x 7" pieces (Front, Back, Roof) and two 5" x 6" pieces (Sides) 14-count antique brown perforated paper from Wichelt Imports Inc.®*
- One skein each DMC® six-strand embroidery floss**
- One spool each Kreinik Very Fine Braid #4**
- Size 24 tapestry needle

*See Sources on page 56.
**Refer to color code.

	DMC®	
■	310	black
✳	3808	turquoise, ul. vy. dk.
·	blanc	white
◑	321	red
○⌈	blanc	white
	743	yellow, med.
@	905	parrot green, dk.
z	470	avocado green, lt.
3	367	pistachio green, dk.
◇	907	parrot green, lt.
#	970	pumpkin, lt.

	Kreinik Very Fine Braid #4	
/	032	pearl
ℓ	5760	marshmallow*

*Two spools required.

Stitch Count
Sides: 35H x 45W each
Front & Back: 47H x 43W each
Roof: 61H x 45W

Design Size
Sides: 2½" x 3¼" each
Front & Back: 3⅜" x 3⅛" each
Roof: 4⅜" x 3¼"

Instructions: Cross stitch over one square using two strands of floss or one strand of very fine braid. When two colors are bracketed together, use one strand of each.

Backstitch over one square using one strand of floss or very fine braid. (**Note:** *Red lines indicate trim lines and are not to be backstitched.*)

Backstitch Instructions
032 inside of peppermint candies
970 snowman's nose
310 remainder of backstitch

Finishing Materials & Instructions
One 8½" x 11" piece brown cardstock
3½" x 3½" piece 14-count antique brown perforated paper
Four 5" x 5" pieces foam-core board
Strong double-stick tape
X-Acto® knife
Double-stick tape
Craft glue

Front

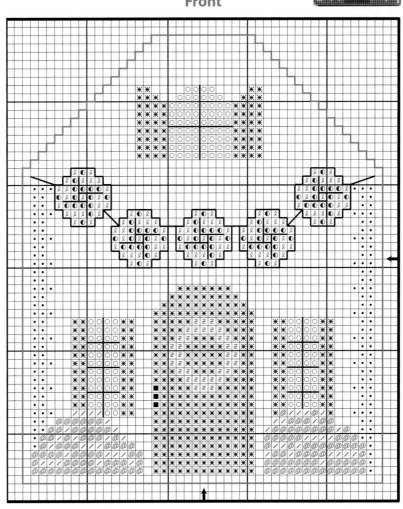

Trim each stitched piece along red lines as indicated on charts. Using trimmed pieces as templates, cut cardstock to same size. Using cardstock pieces as templates, cut two Side and one Front and Back pieces of foam core to same size. Set foam core pieces aside. Glue matching cardstock to the back of each stitched piece.

"Test-fit" cardstock pieces to each piece of foam core to make sure foam core isn't visible beyond stitched piece; trim foam core, if necessary. To assemble foam-core "skeleton" of cottage, align foam-core Front, Back and Sides so that cut edges of Front and Back are inside Side walls at corners; glue walls together at corners and let dry completely or use double-stick tape.

Carefully position stitched pieces on foam-core cube and adhere using double-stick tape. Carefully fold Roof piece in half and position over top of house; glue or tape in place along edges of foam-core cube.

Cut perforated paper piece to fit bottom of cottage (approximate stitch count of 43H x 45W; adjust as needed). Personalize perforated-paper bottom if desired using a favorite cross-stitch alphabet or scrapbook paper. Position piece and glue in place around edges. ✍

Back

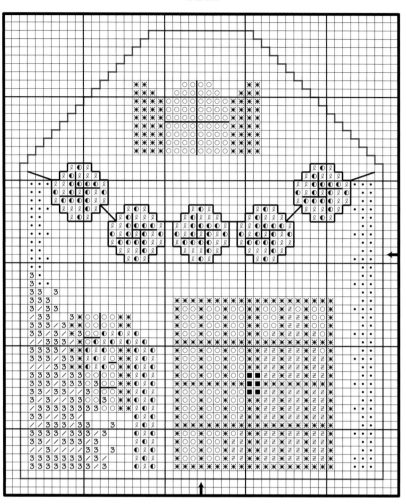

Side One

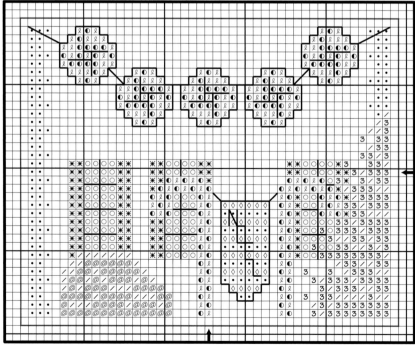

Roof

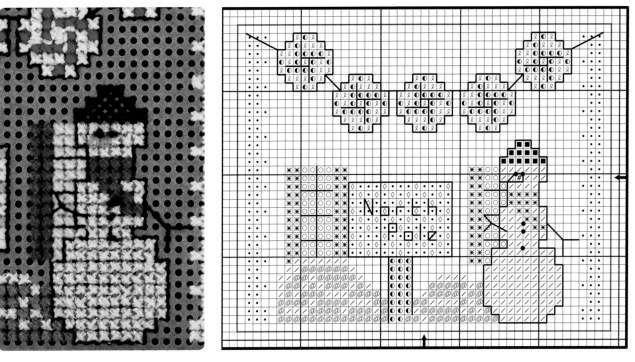

Side Two

How to Stitch

Use the information in this section to help you create the right stitch and select the correct tools to complete your projects.

Working From Charted Designs

A square on a chart corresponds to a space for a cross stitch on the stitching surface. The symbol in a square shows the floss color to be used for the stitch. The width and height for the design stitch area are given in number of stitches and in inches; centers are shown by arrows at bottom and right-hand side of chart. Locations of backstitches and straight stitches are shown by heavy lines, and French knots are shown by dots.

Fabrics

In our materials listings, we give paper suggestions that will complement each design. Our stitched samples were worked on 14-count perforated paper, which have 14 squares per inch; that number is called the thread count.

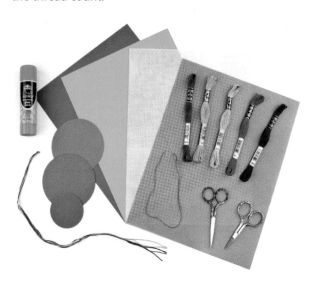

Needles

A blunt-tipped tapestry needle, size 24, is used for stitching on 14-count papers. The correct-size needle is easy to thread with the amount of floss required, but is not so large that it will tear the holes in the paper. When threading needle, insert one end of strand or strands of floss and pull through.

Floss

All of our samples were stitched using cotton or metallic embroidery floss. Color numbers are given for floss. Cut floss into comfortable working lengths; we suggest about 12–18 inches. When separating the strands, gently pull apart the strands and regroup as indicated by pattern (Figure 1).

Fig. 1

Scissors

Good scissors are a necessary stitching tool to have on hand. They are used to cut fabric and floss. We recommend having two pairs of sharp embroidery scissors—one for cutting floss and one for trimming the perforated paper. Always be careful when using sharp scissors or when trimming your designs.

Getting Started

To begin in an unstitched area, bring threaded needle from back through to front of paper (Figure 2). Hold about ¼ inch of the end of the floss against the back and then secure it in place by catching it in the back loops of your first few stitches (Figure 3). To end flosses and begin new ones next to existing stitches, weave through the backs of several stitches. Whenever possible, start stitching in the center of a project as indicated by arrows on charts.

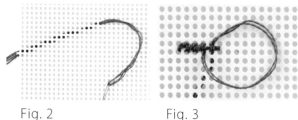

Fig. 2   Fig. 3

The Stitches

The number of strands of floss used for stitching will be determined by the thread count of the fabric or paper used and the pattern. Refer to the chart and instructions to determine the number of strands used for cross stitches or backstitches.

Cross Stitch

A cross stitch is formed in two motions. Following the numbering in Figure 4 below, bring the needle up at 1, down at 2, up at 3 and down at 4 to complete the stitch. Work horizontal rows of stitches wherever possible. Two options exist for stitching: 1) Bring needle up at 1 and down at 2; work half of each stitch across the row, and then complete the stitches on your return; or 2) Bring needle up at 1 and complete each stitch before moving on to the next stitch.

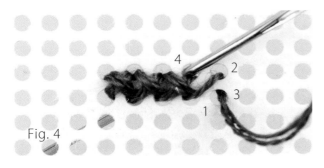

Fig. 4

Backstitch

Backstitches are worked after cross stitches have been completed. They may lie in any direction and are occasionally worked over more than one square of paper. Figure 5 shows the progression of several stitches. Bring the needle up at odd numbers and down at even numbers.

Fig. 5

French Knot

Bring the needle up where indicated on chart. Wrap floss once around needle (Figures 6-8) and reinsert in the same place. Hold wrapped floss tightly and pull needle through, letting floss go just as knot is formed. Pull gently and firmly, but do not pull too tightly.

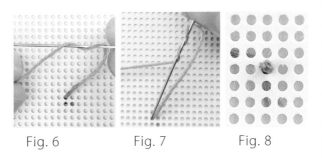

Fig. 6   Fig. 7   Fig. 8

Straight Stitch

Work straight stitches after cross stitches and backstitches have been completed. They may slope in any direction and are typically worked over more than one square of perforated paper. Using the number of strands indicated in the instructions, bring the needle up at odd numbers and down at even numbers (Figure 9).

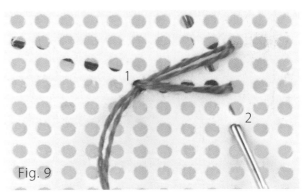

Fig. 9

Planning a Project

Before you stitch, decide how large to cut the paper. Determine the stitched design size and then allow enough additional paper around the design plus 3–5 inches more on each side for use in finishing and mounting if finishing differently than indicated. Try to allow 4 inches extra on each side on perforated paper. Cut your paper exactly true, right along the holes of the paper.

Special Thanks

Designers

Angela Pullen Atherton
Marie Barber
Patti Connor
Donna V. Giampa
Breanne Jackson
Sharon Pope
Christy Schmitz
Elizabeth Spurlock

Stitchers

Meagan Brys
Amanda Fitcher
Cindy Herman
Pamela Kandil
Shirley Meyer
Michelle Munger
Judy Osterhoudt
Wava Rowe
Ann Schmitz
Terri Scott
Connie Winslett
Jane Witt

Model Finishers

Suzanne Herman
Christy Schmitz

Sources

The DMC Corp., 10 Basin Drive, Suite 130, Kearny, NJ 07032, (800) 275-4117, www.dmc-usa.com

The Gentle Art, P.O. Box 670, New Albany, OH 43054-0670, (614) 855-8346, www.thegentleart.com

Kreinik Mfg. Co. Inc., P.O. Box 1966, Parkersburg, WV 26102, (800) 537-2166, www.kreinik.com

Spellbinders Paper Arts, LLC., 1125 W. Pinnacle Peak Road, Bldg 3, Suite 124, Phoenix, AZ 85027, (888) 547-0400, www.spellbinderspaperarts.com

Weeks Dye Works Inc., 1510-103 Mechanical Blvd., Garner, NC 27529-2564, (877) 683-7393, www.weeksdyeworks.com

Wichelt Imports Inc., N162 Highway 35, Stoddard, WI 54658-9711, (800) 356-9516, www.wichelt.com

Yarn Tree, 117 Alexander Ave., Ames, IA 50010, (800) 247-3952, www.yarntree.com

Cross-Stitch Christmas Creations: Festive Perforated Paper Designs is published by Annie's, 306 East Parr Road, Berne, IN 46711. Printed in USA. Copyright © 2014, 2015 Annie's. All rights reserved. This publication may not be reproduced in part or in whole without written permission from the publisher.

RETAIL STORES: If you would like to carry this publication or any other Annie's publication, visit AnniesWSL.com.

Every effort has been made to ensure that the instructions in this publication are complete and accurate. We cannot, however, take responsibility for human error, typographical mistakes or variations in individual work. Please visit AnniesCustomerService.com to check for pattern updates.

ISBN: 978-1-57367-589-5
3 4 5 6 7 8 9 10